The Superstorm
Hurricane Sandy

JOSH GREGORY

Children's Press®
An Imprint of Scholastic Inc.
New York Toronto London Auckland Sydney
Mexico City New Delhi Hong Kong
Danbury, Connecticut

Content Consultant

Jack Williams, founding editor of the *USA Today* weather pages and author of *The AMS Weather Book: The Ultimate Guide to America's Weather*

Library of Congress Cataloging-in-Publication Data

Gregory, Josh.
  The superstorm Sandy / Josh Gregory.
      pages cm.—(A true book)
  Audience: 9–12.
  Audience: Grade 4 to 6.
  Includes bibliographical references and index.
  ISBN 978-0-531-23750-2 (lib. bdg.) — ISBN 978-0-531-23751-9 (pbk.)
1. Hurricane Sandy, 2012—Juvenile literature. 2. Hurricane damage—United States—Juvenile literature. 3. Hurricanes—United States—Juvenile literature. 4. Disaster relief—United States—Juvenile literature. I. Title.
  QC944.2.G74 2013
  363.34'9220974—dc23   2012045292

All rights reserved. Published in 2013 by Children's Press, an imprint of Scholastic Inc.
Printed in China 62
SCHOLASTIC, CHILDREN'S PRESS, A TRUE BOOK, and associated logos are trademarks and/or registered trademarks of Scholastic Inc.
4 5 6 7 8 9 10 R 22 21 20 19 18 17 16 15 14 13

Front cover: Fun Pier roller coaster, Seaside Heights, New Jersey

Front cover inset: Taxis in a flooded Hoboken, New Jersey, parking lot

Back cover: Satellite image of Hurricane Sandy

Find the Truth!

Everything you are about to read is true *except* for one of the sentences on this page.

Which one is **TRUE**?

T or F The effects of Hurricane Sandy were only felt in the northeastern United States.

T or F More than eight million homes and businesses in the United States lost power during the storm.

Find the answers in this book.

Contents

THE **BIG** TRUTH!

Horrible Hurricanes

Sandy's severe weather caused more than 5,000 flights to be canceled in the United States.

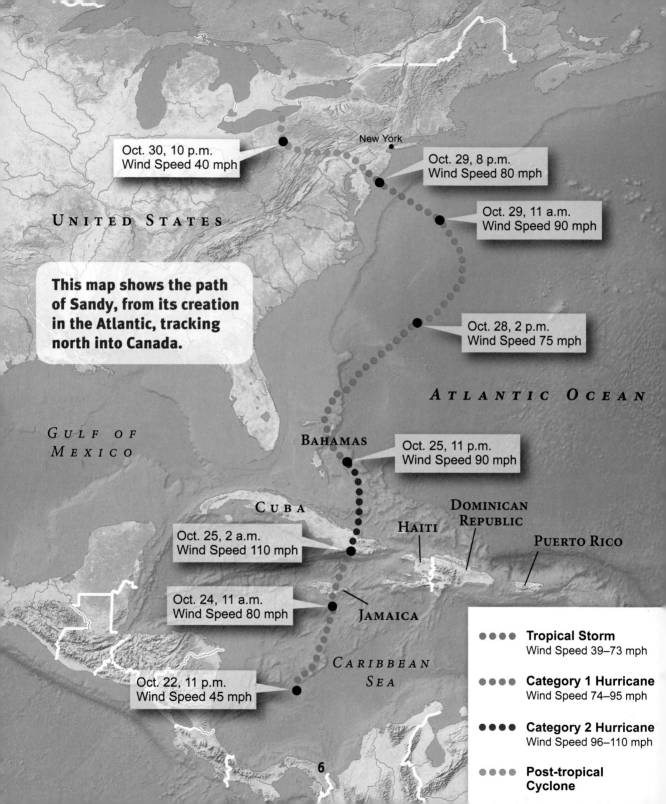

Oct. 30, 10 p.m.
Wind Speed 40 mph

New York

Oct. 29, 8 p.m.
Wind Speed 80 mph

Oct. 29, 11 a.m.
Wind Speed 90 mph

UNITED STATES

This map shows the path
of Sandy, from its creation
in the Atlantic, tracking
north into Canada.

Oct. 28, 2 p.m.
Wind Speed 75 mph

GULF OF
MEXICO

ATLANTIC OCEAN

BAHAMAS

Oct. 25, 11 p.m.
Wind Speed 90 mph

CUBA

DOMINICAN
REPUBLIC

HAITI

PUERTO RICO

Oct. 25, 2 a.m.
Wind Speed 110 mph

Oct. 24, 11 a.m.
Wind Speed 80 mph

JAMAICA

Oct. 22, 11 p.m.
Wind Speed 45 mph

CARIBBEAN
SEA

●●●● Tropical Storm
Wind Speed 39–73 mph

●●●● Category 1 Hurricane
Wind Speed 74–95 mph

●●●● Category 2 Hurricane
Wind Speed 96–110 mph

●●●● Post-tropical
Cyclone

6

CHAPTER 1

Storm on the Horizon

October 2012 will be remembered for one of the most powerful **hurricanes** ever recorded. It cut a path of destruction through the islands of the Caribbean Sea and into the eastern United States. More than 100 people were killed. Countless others lost their homes to wind and floods. It was not the first hurricane to hit the region. However, few hurricanes in the area have caused damage on such a major scale.

Most hurricanes turn east as they move up the U.S. coast but Sandy turned west.

A Storm Forms

Each year, powerful storms develop over the warm tropical portion of the Atlantic Ocean. Some of the most powerful are tropical storms. These are given names to help **meteorologists** keep track of them. On October 22, 2012, a tropical storm developed in waters north of Panama. Meteorologists named it Sandy. Sandy moved north and grew stronger. Five days after forming, its winds reached speeds of 74 miles per hour (119 kilometers per hour), officially making it a hurricane.

Sandy became a tropical storm as it moved from the Atlantic Ocean over the Caribbean Sea.

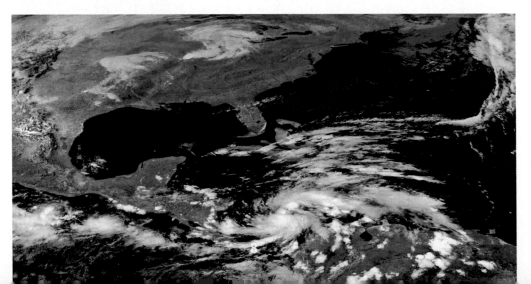

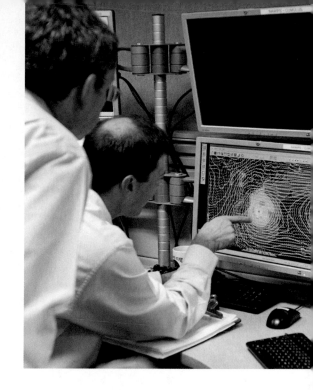

Meteorologists carefully tracked Sandy's progress.

Something Special

Several hurricanes occur each year, but Sandy was different. Ten days after it formed, the hurricane combined with another storm system. This made it an extratropical hurricane. Tropical storms get energy from warm ocean waters. Extratropical storms draw energy from contrasts between warm and cold temperatures in the atmosphere. Sandy not only became stronger, but also bigger. Powerful winds blew 420 miles (676 km) from the storm's center. Such winds extend fewer than 300 miles (483 km) in a typical hurricane. Newscasters dubbed Sandy a "superstorm."

Workers in Jamaica try to stand a utility line back up after it was blown over when Sandy passed through.

The First Strike

Even before becoming a superstorm, Sandy was powerful. On October 24, it made its first **landfall** in Jamaica. Sandy battered the island nation with powerful winds and heavy rain. It drove thousands of residents and tourists into shelters and hotels. More than 70 percent of the country lost power. One man was killed when a boulder crushed his home. Though there were no other **casualties**, mudslides and floods brought on by Sandy's rain damaged many homes, businesses, and other structures.

No Sign of Stopping

After making landfall in Jamaica, Sandy made its way to other nearby nations. Haiti was hit especially hard. More than 200,000 Haitians were driven from their homes as the southern part of the country experienced significant flooding. At least 54 people died during the storm. Many Haitians were still homeless from a massive earthquake that had struck in 2010. They had only tents to protect them from the fierce storm.

Two children sit on a cot in their home, which was flooded by Sandy, in Port-au-Prince, Haiti.

Floodwaters washed away entire streets in Port-au-Prince, Haiti.

To the west, the storm reached the Cuban coast near the city of Santiago. More than 15,000 homes were destroyed. Sandy's winds tore away roofs and sent trees smashing into walls. Eleven people were killed. Huge portions of the country went days without gas, electricity, or clean water.

Just east of Haiti, the Dominican Republic and Puerto Rico also experienced Hurricane Sandy firsthand. Two Dominicans and one Puerto Rican were killed in the storm.

A man digs through the wreckage of his home in Aguacate, Cuba, after Hurricane Sandy destroyed the building.

A Changing Climate

Over the past century, Earth's average temperature has steadily increased. This global warming has led to climate change, which has been made worse by pollution and other human activities.

One result of climate change seems to be extremely strong weather events. Many experts agree that some effects of global warming helped make Sandy so powerful. If climate change continues at its current rate, we could see other disastrous weather events in the future.

Battering the Bahamas

Sandy continued its destructive path through the Caribbean and over the Atlantic Ocean. The storm moved north toward the Bahamas. This nation is made up of hundreds of individual islands. By the time the storm neared the capital city of Nassau, Sandy's winds had reached speeds of around 100 miles per hour (161 kph). One person died as the storm made its way through the islands. Significant damage was done to buildings and other structures.

Timeline of Sandy

October 24
Tropical Storm Sandy becomes a hurricane and hits Jamaica.

October 25
Hurricane Sandy hits Cuba, Haiti, the Dominican Republic, and Puerto Rico.

Ups and Downs

The day after making its way through the Bahamas, Sandy's wind speeds began to die down. Briefly, it was once again a tropical storm instead of a hurricane. But as it continued its northward path, it picked up speed. Sandy soon returned to hurricane levels. People in the United States began to fear the worst. Sandy grew in size and strength on October 29, when it combined with a second storm system. The superstorm then turned west, heading straight for New Jersey.

October 26
Sandy strikes the Bahamas.

October 27
Sandy is briefly downgraded to a tropical storm, but soon speeds up to become a hurricane once more.

October 29
Sandy reaches the East Coast of the United States.

U.S. president Barack Obama worked to help prepare the United States for the storm as Sandy approached.

CHAPTER 2

Plans and Preparations

With Sandy drawing closer, people in the United States began bracing themselves. On October 28, President Barack Obama signed emergency declarations. These provided government resources to states in the storm's path. The resources helped state officials prepare for Sandy's arrival.

The following day, Obama addressed the nation. He discussed the storm and the government's plan for providing relief. "Our number one priority is to make sure we are saving lives," he said.

Leaving Everything Behind

Government officials issued **evacuation** orders to many people living on or near the coastline. These areas would likely experience severe flooding. People in low **elevations** along the coast were especially at risk. Hundreds of thousands of people packed clothing and important possessions. They left their homes in New York, New Jersey, and Connecticut. Some people were lucky enough to find hotel rooms or stay with friends and relatives. Others waited out the storm in community shelters.

The American Red Cross and other organizations opened shelters to people evacuating from areas in Hurricane Sandy's path.

People in Jersey City, New Jersey, fill sandbags with sand provided by the Army Corps of Engineers.

Boarding Up the House

Even in areas less likely to experience severe flooding, government organizations and private citizens prepared for the storm. They built sandbag walls against doors and around tunnels to help keep water out. Many people boarded up their windows. This would help protect against flying objects that might break the glass. People who kept boats along the coast moved them to safer locations. Some people cut down trees so storm winds wouldn't fling them into buildings or power lines.

Many stores experienced a shortage of basic supplies such as bottled water as people tried to stock up in preparation for Sandy.

Holing Up at Home

People who hadn't been evacuated from their homes began preparing to ride out the storm. They flocked to local grocery stores for supplies. Store shelves were soon emptied of bread, canned goods, and bottled water. Some people made sure to have gas-powered **generators** ready. These would be useful in case of power outages. Other people gathered batteries, radios, and flashlights. Officials warned that it would be dangerous to go outdoors once the storm hit.

Going Nowhere

Government officials encouraged people not to travel during the storm. They ordered everyone to stay off the highways that meteorologists predicted would be affected. New York City's subway system was closed down, and all flights into and out of the region were canceled. Many schools and businesses also closed. This helped make sure students and workers were not caught outside during a commute when the storm hit.

New York City's subways remained closed for several days. People could not get to work or school.

Even with all the preparations, subways filled with water and were severely damaged.

Horrible Hurricanes

Sandy was not the first hurricane to barrel down on the United States. Each storm is a learning experience that helps us to protect ourselves better against the next one.

THE GREAT NEW ENGLAND HURRICANE

This deadly storm hit Long Island, New York, on September 21, 1938. There was almost no warning. Meteorologists had lost track of the storm after it passed North Carolina earlier in the day. As it swept northward, 700 people were killed. The damage equaled about $18 billion in today's dollars. Since then, weather tracking technology has greatly improved. Meteorologists also work hard to keep the public informed of potentially severe weather.

HURRICANE HAZEL

On October 15, 1954, Hazel came ashore near Myrtle Beach, South Carolina. It then made its way north along the coast. The storm killed 22 people and caused millions of dollars of damage. Like Sandy, Hazel combined forces with another storm system. It turned into an extratropical nightmare after it moved inland. The level of destruction spawned a wave of research into how hurricanes work, leading to more accurate weather predictions years later.

HURRICANE KATRINA

This hurricane was one of the deadliest, most destructive storms ever recorded. Katrina laid waste to cities and towns along the coast of the Gulf of Mexico in August 2005. Hundreds of thousands of people lost their homes. More than 1,800 people died. As of 2012, many areas along the Gulf Coast had yet to fully recover from Katrina's effects. Scientists, government officials, and the public are still learning from Katrina. More effective flood prevention and evacuation efforts are among the issues people are working on.

City officials closed off the area around the dangling crane in New York City.

24

CHAPTER 3

Winds and Waters

Sandy had grown so powerful that its effects could be felt long before it made landfall. On the morning of Monday, October 29, ocean waters surged up the coastline. City streets and buildings became flooded. Wild winds bent trees and sent loose objects flying. In New York City, the arm of a skyscraper construction crane bent backward in the wind. It dangled 70 stories above the sidewalk. Authorities ordered an emergency evacuation of the area.

The skyscraper, named One57, will be New York's tallest residential building once finished.

Landfall

Early signs of the storm continued all day. People began to dread what would happen as Sandy crashed ashore. At around 8:00 p.m., the massive storm's eye hit land near Atlantic City, New Jersey. As Sandy crossed over the coastline, its fastest winds were clocked at 80 miles per hour (129 kph). Winds and flooding affected areas from Virginia to New England. People throughout the entire northeastern region stayed inside their homes, hoping the storm would end soon.

Atlantic City, New Jersey, suffered heavy flooding, which covered streets and closed off neighborhoods.

Flooding was made worse by a full moon, which causes a month's highest tides.

Water flooded this fleet of taxis in Hoboken, New Jersey, when Sandy hit.

Waves in the Streets

Floodwaters roared through streets in the most heavily affected areas. Cars floated up from underground flooded parking garages. Fourteen-foot (4-meter) waves were sighted offshore from New York City. Subway tunnels filled with water, causing the worst devastation to New York's subway system in 100 years. The system wouldn't be usable for days. In Connecticut, floodwaters swept through a **sewage** treatment plant. Thousands of gallons of harmful wastewater were washed into surrounding towns, increasing the risk of disease among residents.

Nearly 200 firefighters worked to put out the Breezy Point fire.

Devastation

Many buildings hit by the worst parts of the storm were unable to hold up against the devastating winds and waters. A fire broke out overnight in the Breezy Point area of Queens, New York. Sandy's winds carried the flames, spreading them through the entire neighborhood. Fire trucks could not reach the fire because of flooded roads. More than 100 homes had been destroyed by the time the blaze was put out in the morning.

In the Dark

To make matters worse, millions of people weathered the storm in total darkness. Water flooded into **substations**. Power companies were forced to shut down electricity throughout the Northeast to avoid damaging the systems. At the same time, wind and debris knocked down power and phone lines. Around 8.5 million homes and businesses were left in a blackout at the storm's peak.

In spite of people's preparations, floodwaters damaged electrical equipment in New York City's substations.

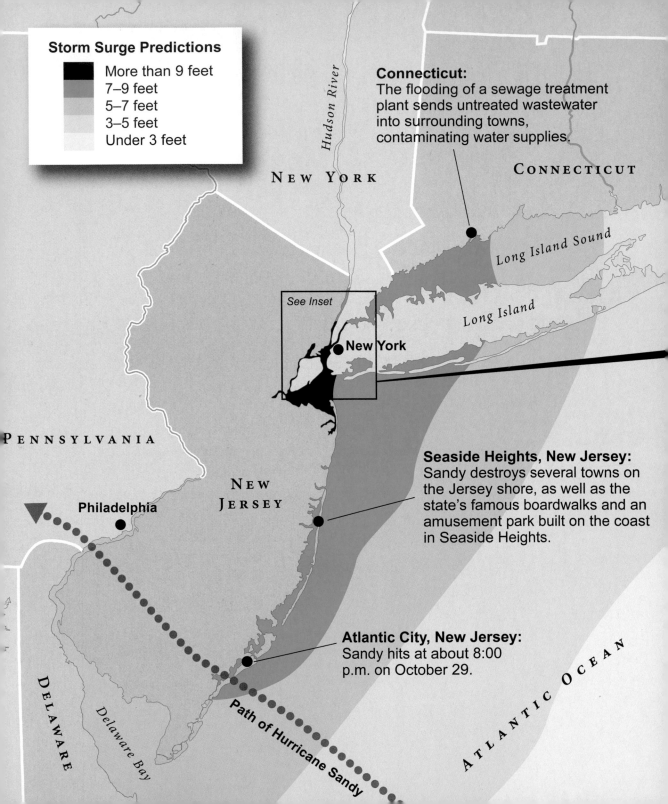

Storm Surge Predictions

- More than 9 feet
- 7–9 feet
- 5–7 feet
- 3–5 feet
- Under 3 feet

Hudson River

NEW YORK

Connecticut:
The flooding of a sewage treatment plant sends untreated wastewater into surrounding towns, contaminating water supplies.

CONNECTICUT

Long Island Sound

Long Island

See Inset

New York

PENNSYLVANIA

Philadelphia

NEW JERSEY

Seaside Heights, New Jersey:
Sandy destroys several towns on the Jersey shore, as well as the state's famous boardwalks and an amusement park built on the coast in Seaside Heights.

Atlantic City, New Jersey:
Sandy hits at about 8:00 p.m. on October 29.

DELAWARE

Delaware Bay

Path of Hurricane Sandy

ATLANTIC OCEAN

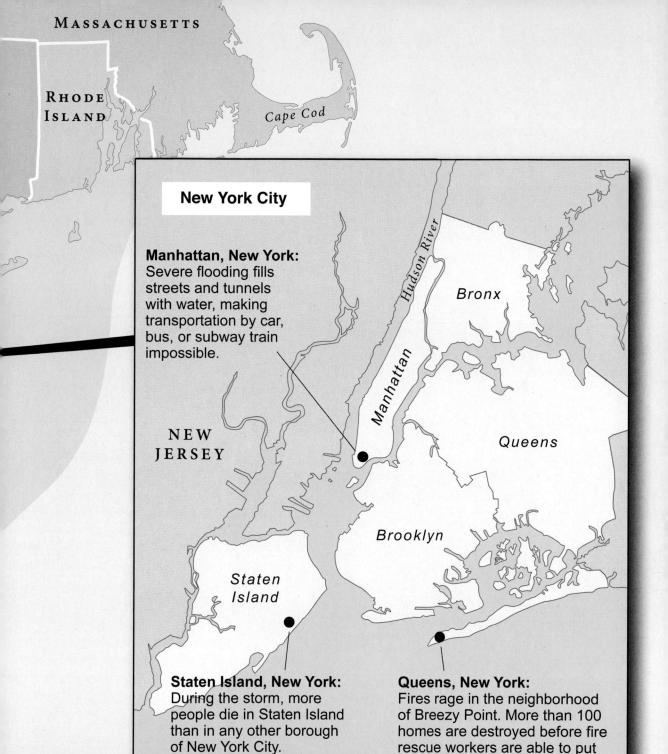

MASSACHUSETTS

RHODE
ISLAND

Cape Cod

New York City

Manhattan, New York:
Severe flooding fills
streets and tunnels
with water, making
transportation by car,
bus, or subway train
impossible.

Hudson River

Bronx

Manhattan

Queens

NEW
JERSEY

Brooklyn

*Staten
Island*

Staten Island, New York:
During the storm, more
people die in Staten Island
than in any other borough
of New York City.

Queens, New York:
Fires rage in the neighborhood
of Breezy Point. More than 100
homes are destroyed before fire
rescue workers are able to put
the flames out.

31

Rescue workers with boats made their way through flooded streets to help residents.

CHAPTER 4

After the Storm

By the next morning, rescue workers had begun to search through damaged buildings for people who had been trapped or injured. Many rescue workers had to travel through the city streets in boats. Utility workers set out immediately to begin restoring electricity and other important services. At the same time, thousands of people in shelters waited to hear if their homes were still standing.

Workers used boats to rescue not only people, but also pets.

The Storm's Terrible Toll

By the end of the week, the extent of Sandy's impact became clear. More than 100 people had been killed. A man from Staten Island, New York, drowned in his basement. He had gotten his family safely to the attic, the highest part of the house. A downed power line electrocuted one woman. Another woman suffered a heart attack after a power outage turned off the respirator she relied on to help her breathe.

A group of medical workers takes a newborn baby onto an ambulance in New York City. The hospital had to be evacuated during Sandy.

Sandy made roads as far south as North Carolina impassable. →

Out of Service

Millions of survivors were stuck for days without important resources. Without electricity or phones, many people were unable to call friends and relatives to let them know they were safe. People who could reach gas stations stood in line for hours to fill containers with fuel to power home generators. Even some people who had power were forced to stay in their homes. This was because roads and public transportation systems remained closed. Slowly, though, people began surveying the damage around them.

Residents grill food for the neighborhood on the streets of New York City after the storm.

Hungry and Thirsty

Floods had ruined food supplies in grocery stores and restaurants. Many roads were closed, so delivery trucks could not get through. As a result, food and drinking water shortages developed in some areas. There were a few restaurants and food trucks that were able to open in New York and New Jersey. These provided some people nearby with a hot meal when they couldn't cook at home. Other people fired up grills on city sidewalks, bypassing the need for gasoline or electricity.

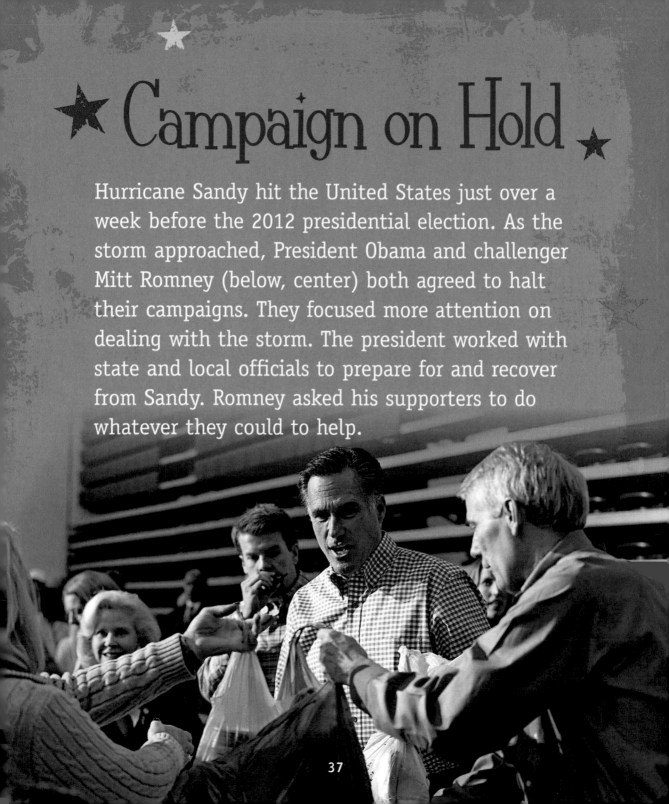

★ Campaign on Hold ★

Hurricane Sandy hit the United States just over a week before the 2012 presidential election. As the storm approached, President Obama and challenger Mitt Romney (below, center) both agreed to halt their campaigns. They focused more attention on dealing with the storm. The president worked with state and local officials to prepare for and recover from Sandy. Romney asked his supporters to do whatever they could to help.

Far, Far Away

Sandy's effects were even felt hundreds of miles from where the storm hit. Midwestern states such as Wisconsin and Illinois experienced high winds. People living near Lake Michigan were warned of potential surges. On local beaches in Connecticut, cleanup workers discovered bird species from Europe and the Arctic. They had been dragged all the way to Connecticut by Sandy's winds.

Waves as high as 20 feet (6 m) on Lake Michigan were reported in Chicago, Illinois.

Sandy plowed a path across Mantoloking, New Jersey, located on a narrow strip of land extending into the Atlantic Ocean.

Changing the World

Some of Sandy's effects are likely to be permanent. **Erosion** is expected to change the shape of beaches along the coasts of places such as New York and New Jersey. Surging waters also dragged huge amounts of sand inland. The sand formed hills called dunes. On Long Island, New York, floodwaters formed new **inlets**. Experts believe that these new bodies of water may be a lasting addition to the land.

President Barack Obama (seated, left) and New Jersey governor Chris Christie (standing, behind) speak with Superstorm Sandy survivors.

CHAPTER 5

The Long Road to Recovery

People look to their state and local leaders after a devastating event such as Superstorm Sandy. New Jersey governor Chris Christie rationed gasoline and worked so residents could regain electricity. New York City's mayor Michael Bloomberg helped implement a plan to gradually get public transportation running again. In Connecticut, Governor Dannel Malloy shut down state highways to keep people safe. Mayor Cory Booker of Newark, New Jersey, opened his home to people to charge their phones and even sleep in his extra beds while he dealt with the storm.

Relief on Its Way

Relief organizations sprang into action following the storm. The Federal Emergency Management Agency (FEMA) dedicated resources to cleanup and rebuilding. With the Red Cross and Salvation Army, FEMA also provided food, water, and other supplies to those in need. Large companies donated millions of dollars. Small businesses and schools around the country collected supplies. Four days after the storm, NBC hosted a concert. Its performers encouraged viewers to donate to the Red Cross.

Red Cross workers visit residents of Staten Island, New York, after the storm.

Residents and rescue workers continued to assess the damage caused by Superstorm Sandy in Breezy Point in Queens, New York, and elsewhere for days after the storm passed.

Getting Better

Sandy caused widespread, serious damage. Rebuilding will not be an easy or fast process. Disasters of this scale can impact a region for years. For example, people living in New Orleans, Louisiana, still confront the lasting evidence of Hurricane Katrina years after it hit the city in 2005. The region affected by Superstorm Sandy will heal over time. But it will never forget the events of October 29, 2012. ★

True Statistics

Height of highest recorded waves caused by Sandy: 39.7 ft. (12.1 m) off the New Jersey coast

Speed of highest recorded wind gusts caused by Sandy: Around 100 mph (161 kph)

Estimated damage caused by Sandy in the United States: More than $25 billion

Estimated damage caused along the Gulf Coast by Hurricane Katrina: $81 billion

Number of deaths in the United States caused by Sandy: At least 100

Number of deaths outside the United States caused by Sandy: At least 68

Number of deaths caused by Hurricane Katrina: More than 1,800

Number of people without power one week after Sandy: About 1.4 million

Did you find the truth?

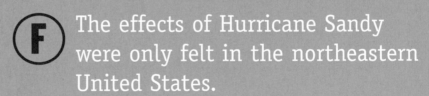

F The effects of Hurricane Sandy were only felt in the northeastern United States.

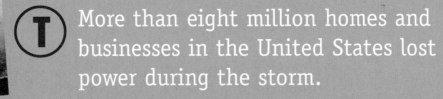

T More than eight million homes and businesses in the United States lost power during the storm.

Resources

Books

Benoit, Peter. *Hurricane Katrina*. New York: Children's Press, 2012.

Carson, Mary Kay. *Inside Hurricanes*. New York: Sterling, 2010.

Park, Louise. *Hurricanes*. North Mankato, MN: Smart Apple Media, 2008.

Silverstein, Alvin. *Hurricanes: The Science Behind Killer Storms*. Berkeley Heights, NJ: Enslow Publishers, 2010.

Visit this Scholastic Web site for more information on Superstorm Sandy:
★ www.factsfornow.scholastic.com
Enter the keywords **Superstorm Sandy**

Important Words

casualties (KAZH-uhl-teez) — people who are injured or killed in an accident, natural disaster, or war

elevations (el-uh-VAY-shuhnz) — heights above sea level

erosion (i-ROH-zhuhn) — the wearing away of something by water or wind

evacuation (i-vak-yoo-A-shuhn) — the movement away from a building or area because it is dangerous there

generators (JEN-uh-ray-turz) — machines that produce electricity by turning a magnet inside a coil of wire

hurricanes (HUR-ih-canez) — violent storms with heavy rain and winds 74 miles per hour or greater (119 kph)

inlets (IN-lets) — narrow bodies of water that lead inland from a larger body of water, such as an ocean, lake, or river

landfall (LAND-fawl) — the time and place when a hurricane over an ocean hits land

meteorologists (mee-tee-uh-RAH-luh-jists) — experts in the study of Earth's atmosphere

sewage (SOO-ij) — liquid and solid waste that is carried off by sewers and drains

substations (SUHB-stay-shuhnz) — systems that help control the flow of electricity from power plants to homes and businesses

Index

Page numbers in **bold** indicate illustrations

About the Author

Josh Gregory writes and edits books for kids. He lives in Chicago, Illinois.

DISCARD